Great Fire of London

Workbook

By Sarah Lee

Contents

Fill in the Missing Words

Using the words below fill in the missing words.

bricks   Pudding Lane   four   wood   blow   leather

The fire began in ....

It spread quickly because the houses were made of ....

The fire lasted for .... days.

They used .... buckets filled with water.

They had to .... up the buildings to stop the fire.

After the fire they made the houses from ....

LONDON ON FIRE

The fire began in the baker's shop in Pudding Lane at 1am on 2nd September 1666. Due to the hot dry summer London have had this year, the wooden houses were very dry, and caught fire easily. The houses being so close together, and with many roofs being thatched, caused the fire to rage out of control. A strong westerly wind has blown the fire westwards towards the London Bridge, and is now threatening the Tower of London. Thomas Bludworth the Mayor of London is saying the fire is not as serious as people are making out, and when questioned did not believe the houses should be demolished to stop the fire spreading. King Charles was unavailable for comment. People are fleeing their homes and heading towards the river. Samuel Pepy's a senior Royal Navy official said he was having dinner when he noticed London on fire. He hired a boat and sailed down the river to take a closer look, and was horrified at the damage that was being done, and there was no end to the fire, it is still raging. Samuel said he was surprised everyone were intent on saving their belongings, but nobody was trying to put the fire out.

William Hunt, who lived in Pudding Lane described how he was awoken by the sound of Bells. 'I was sleeping, it was around one o'clock in the morning when I first heard the bells, I thought I was dreaming, then I noticed my bedroom was brightly lit, and heard screams and yells coming from the street. I looked out of the window and couldn't believe my eyes. The whole street was alight and people were running down the street towards the river. I woke my wife and we quickly got out, thank God for the bells.'

The fire is getting dangerously close to our offices. Outside our window we can see people with leather buckets pouring water on the flames. Some are using hand squirts and some with long hooks are pulling down burning buildings. Horses and carts are piled high with boxes rugs and mattresses .
The sky is black with smoke and it is so thick it is blocking out the sunlight. Ash and soot are falling like black snow.

We still don't know of the number of dead yet. We hope to keep you updated if we are still here tomorrow.

Write Your own News Report

THE LONDON GAZETTE

3rd September 1666   2d

Great Fire of London Play

Act one can be used as a drama lesson using five characters, Thomas Farryner, his daughter Hannah, his assistant and son Tom his maid Betty and the Narrator. Using bread buns as a prop. Practice in fives and perform your act to an audience then plan Act Two and how you would write it.

Characters:

Narrator
Thomas Farryner (Baker)
Tom (Son and assistant)
Hannah (Daughter)
Betty(Maid)

Act One.

Thomas is upstairs getting ready for bed and shouts downstairs to Tom, Hannah, and Betty who are finishing baking the bread.

THOMAS FARRYNER	Tom, don't forget to close the window and make sure the coals are out before you go to bed. Girls it's getting late, time for bed.
TOM	Of course Father, just finishing the buns.
HANNAH	We will be up soon Father, just cleaning the benches.
BETTY	I think those benches are clean enough, fit for a king.
HANNAH	Come on Betty, bedtime. I am sure the King will be very pleased with his buns Tom, they look perfect. How long will you be?

TOM

Another ten minutes or so. You two go up, I'll see you tomorrow, goodnight girls.

HANNAH AND BETTY

Goodnight Tom.

The two girls run upstairs and get ready for bed. Thomas is already snoring in his bed. Tom is still busy in the kitchen, putting the buns in a basket.

Tom begins to yawn and stretches his arms. He rubs his eyes and begins climbing the stairs to bed. He forgets to close the window or put out the coals.

NARRATOR

A strong gust of wind blows through the window and knocks one of the hot coals in the oven onto the wooden floor. It begins to smoulder.

Thick black smoke rises and flames begin to burn the wooden furniture. Soon the whole of the downstairs is on fire, and the flames begin creeping up the stairs.

Thomas wakes up coughing.

THOMAS FARRYNER

Cough cough! What the!

Thomas runs out of the room, he starts coughing he can't get his breath. The flames are nearly at the top of the stairs. He drops down on his knees where there is less smoke.

THOMAS FARRYNER

Tom! Hannah! Betty! There's a fire! Wake up wake up! Oh No!

Tom, Hannah and Betty run onto the landing coughing.

THOMAS FARRYNER Quick, we need to get on the roof.

They all climb out of the window and onto the roof. Betty clings onto the chimney, she is scared and is crying. Tom jumps onto the roof next door, followed by Hannah.

TOM   Jump Father! Jump Betty!

Thomas leaps onto the roof and nearly falls off. Tom grabs his hand and helps him onto the roof.

Betty clings to the chimney afraid to move. The flames were now licking through the roof.

THOMAS, TOM, HANNAH   Jump Betty, Jump!

Betty just clung onto the chimney shaking her head.

BETTY   I can't, I can't!

NARRATOR

Suddenly the roof caved in, Betty fell into the flames and disappeared.

Act Two

Now plan act two. What happened to the family after this? Where did they go? How did they warn the others in the street?

Write act two in a similar format as above. Then act it out in front of an audience.

UK Map

Colour the London circle red.

Colour the Manchester circle brown.

Colour the Edinburgh circle yellow.

Colour the Glasgow circle blue.

Colour the Dublin circle green.

N _ _ _ _ _ _ _ _ _
I _ _ _ _ _ _ _

S _ _ _ _ _ _ _ _

W _ _ _ _ _

E _ _ _ _ _ _ _ _

Label the map putting the countries, England, Scotland, Wales, and Northern Ireland.

Label the Capital City of London.

Colour England green, Scotland blue, Wales red, and Northern Ireland yellow.

The World

Find the United Kingdom in Europe and colour it Green

Colour the other parts of a map then make a key to show which colours the continents are.

KEY

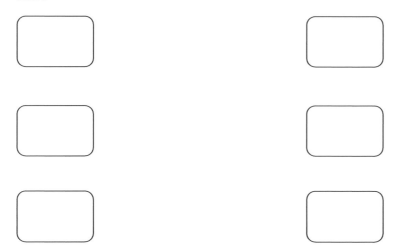

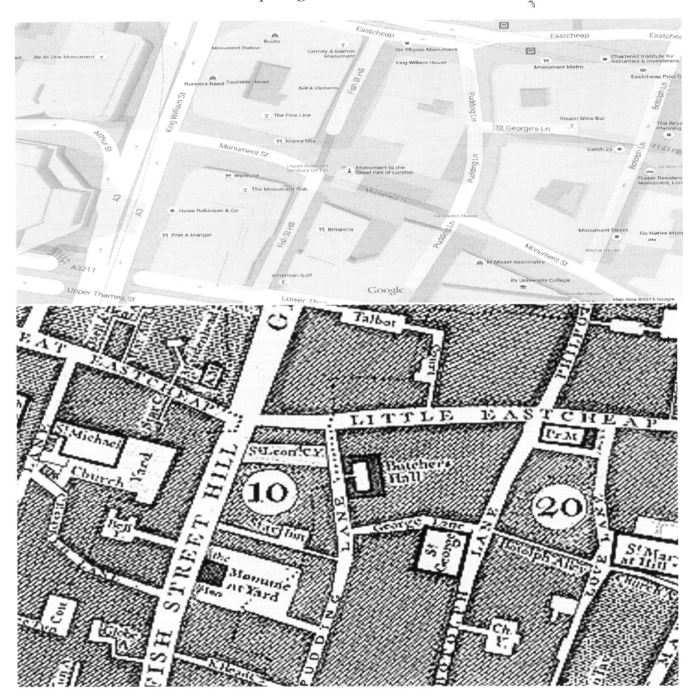

Discuss the differences between the old and new map of London.
Colour Pudding Lane on both maps.
What has changed and what has stayed the same?

Sketch the picture of the Tudor house.

Great Fire of London Haiku

Enormous the flames,
Lit the dark sky in London.
The church bells rang out.

Running for their lives,
The people fled their homes.
The fire spread quickly.

Tinder box houses,
They easily caught fire.
London was burning.

Haiku poems have three lines.
- Line 1 has 5 syllables.
- Line 2 has 7 syllables
- Line 3 has 5 syllables.
- Now try writing your own Haiku poem about The Great Fire of London

_____

_____

_____

_____

_____

_____

_____

_____

_____

_____

_____

_____

Story Writing

The Great Fire of London

**Thomas Farryner   September 2nd 1666   Pudding Lane   London   Samuel Pepy's
King Charles II   hand squirts   leather buckets   demolished   homeless   Christopher
Wren**

Using the picture and the words above for ideas, write your own story about
The Great Fire of London.

_____

_____

_____

_____

_____

_____

_____

_____

_____

_____

_____

_____

_____

_____

Comprehension

On September 1st 1666, in Pudding Lane in London, Thomas Farryner finished baking the bread for the King's men, and went to bed, very tired. He was so tired he forgot to check the oven's fire was out, and due to the hot dry summer they were having, left the window open. The next day, in the early hours of Sunday Morning on September 2nd 1666, Whilst he and his family were sleeping a draft ignited the red hot coals in the oven and started to burn brightly. Soon the kitchen was on fire, flames licked up the stairs towards the bedrooms. Thomas woke up and started coughing with the thick black smoke that had entered his room. He woke his family and his maid and told everyone to climb onto the roof, as their escape down the stairs was impossible. They all climbed onto the roof. Thomas knew if they stayed there they would be in danger, so he told everyone to jump onto the roof next door. The wooden framed houses were very close together, so Thomas his son and daughter jumped onto the roof next door. Betty his maid was afraid, and clung to the chimney afraid to jump. 'Jump!' They all shouted. But Betty just stood there motionless afraid to move. Suddenly, the building collapsed underneath her and she fell through the roof to her death.

Thomas and his family managed to escape, they ran through the streets shouting 'Fire! Fire!' People looked out of their windows in dismay. The dark sky was bright with the flames, black smoke towered above them. Soon other houses caught fire, and within minutes the whole street was on fire. The church bells began to ring to warn the people, and everyone rushed out into the street. They knew their homes were at risk, and all their belongings, so everyone started to collect their belongings from their homes, and using wheelbarrows and carts started to move their belongings away from the fire.

A strong wind was fanning the flames and pushing the fire westwards towards London Bridge. By Monday morning the fire had destroyed three hundred homes and had destroyed London Bridge.

Samuel Pepy's was an important man in the King's navy, and began keeping a diary of what was happening. He wrote that people were fleeing their homes, rescuing their belongings, but nobody seemed to be trying to tackle the fire. Samuel went to find the King, King Charles II, he advised him to pull down some buildings to try and stop the fire spreading. But the king did nothing.

On Tuesday the fire had been burning for two days, and it lit the night sky making it look like daylight. Some people tried to pour water on the fire, but by then it was too hot to get close enough to douse the flames. They used leather buckets filled with water to throw on the fire, some also had hand squirts, which were huge metal syringes, they sucked up water then squirted it on the fire, others used hooks to pull down the burning buildings. Nothing seemed to be working, and the fire was getting closer to the Tower of London. King Charles and his men also got involved in trying to put out the fire.

Some people who had horses and carts jumped at the opportunity to start charging huge fees to help people move their belongings. But soon so many carts started heading towards the London Gate that they blocked the exit, leaving the King no alternative but to close the gate.

Some people ran to St Paul's Cathedral, hoping they would be safe, because the building was made from stone. But they were not safe. The wooden roof of St Paul's caught fire and crashed down onto some people below.

On Wednesday, the King ordered that buildings be demolished to create a gap between the fire and the Tower of London. They used gun powder to blow up the houses. The fire was eventually brought under control. In the four days it burned, it destroyed four hundred streets, thirteen thousand two hundred houses, and eighty seven churches. St Paul's Cathedral was badly damaged, but the King had a plan to rebuild it.

It was hard to know how many people died, because they did not keep many records in those days.

Many people were now homeless and were living in tents on surrounding fields. Samuel Pepy's had written that some of the rich with pianos had managed to rescue them, so even though they were sad they had lost their homes, they still had their music.

After the fire, new rules were made; houses were to be further apart and to be made from brick and stone. They were not allowed to have thatched roofs which caught fire easily. The King asked Christopher Wren, a famous architect to design a new London. He came up with a fabulous design that would have made London look more modern than Paris. But there was not enough funds, or time to use his designs, so instead the King ordered that people rebuilt their properties in the same place where they were before.

New firefighting equipment was ordered so more was available in case it happened again, and horse drawn fire engines were supplied.

A monument designed by Christopher Wren was erected near Pudding lane to serve as a reminder of the terrible event. St Paul's Cathedral was redesigned by Christopher Wren, and it was given its famous dome roof we can see today.

Christopher Wren's monument is still standing today.

Today London is a different safer place with its wide streets, brick and stones buildings and a very efficient Fire service.

Right - St Paul's Cathedral today. Below - the Tower of London today.

1. Where did the fire start?

....

....

2. On what day did the fire start and how long did it last?

....

....

....

3. Who began keeping a diary?

....

....

4. Why did the fire spread so quickly?

....

....

....

....

5. What equipment was used to put out the fires?

....

....

....

....

6. Who was on the throne at the time?

....

....

7. What did they do to stop the fire spreading in the end?

....

....

....

....

8. Who designed the Monument to the Great Fire and the new St Paul's Cathedral?

....

....

....

9. Which famous bridge was burnt down?

....

....

10. What else was destroyed during the fire?

....

....

....

....

10. What changes were made after the fire?

....

....

....

....

....

....

....

....

....

Draw a Picture of a Part of the Story.

Using the pictures, write the story of 'The Great Fire of London'.

Christopher Wren

Using the internet, find out 4 facts about the life of Christopher Wren and his importance during The Great Fire of London.

1...
....
....
2...
....
....
.3...
....
....
.4...
....
....

St Paul's Cathedral

The image above shows St Paul's Cathedral which was newly designed by Christopher Wren after the fire. Copy the image below.

The Great Fire of London

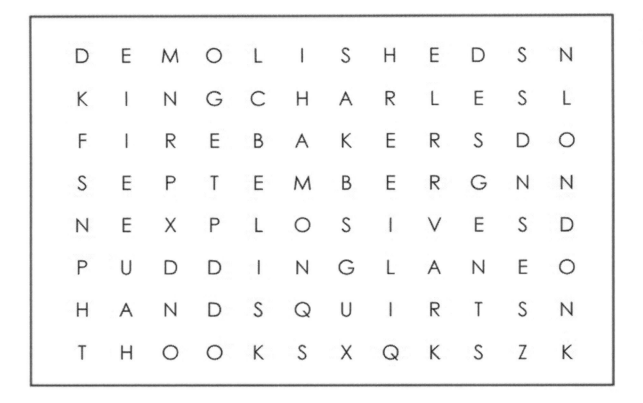

```
D  E  M  O  L  I  S  H  E  D  S  N
K  I  N  G  C  H  A  R  L  E  S  L
F  I  R  E  B  A  K  E  R  S  D  O
S  E  P  T  E  M  B  E  R  G  N  N
N  E  X  P  L  O  S  I  V  E  S  D
P  U  D  D  I  N  G  L  A  N  E  O
H  A  N  D  S  Q  U  I  R  T  S  N
T  H  O  O  K  S  X  Q  K  S  Z  K
```

Find the following words in the puzzle.
Words are hidden → and ↓ .

BAKERS   HANDSQUIRTS   PUDDINGLANE
DEMOLISHED   HOOKS   SEPTEMBER
EXPLOSIVES   KING CHARLES
FIRE   LONDON

The Great Fire of London

```
E  Z  K  I  L  O  N  D  O  N  Q  O  K  B  K  B  I  K
E  X  P  L  O  S  I  V  E  S  D  W  B  J  T  N  N  M
M  L  E  A  T  H  E  R  B  U  C  K  E  T  S  Q  V  S
K  I  N  G  C  H  A  R  L  E  S  D  T  F  R  V  S  Y
Z  D  U  Q  S  A  M  U  E  L  P  E  P  Y  S  S  U  R
N  N  W  S  V  N  Q  O  E  H  O  O  K  S  B  B  V  I
T  A  T  H  O  M  A  S  B  L  U  D  W  O  R  T  H  N
O  B  A  K  E  R  S  Y  S  M  P  H  M  A  Y  O  R  G
C  H  R  I  S  T  O  P  H  E  R  W  R  E  N  S  V  E
E  T  I  H  A  N  D  S  Q  U  I  R  T  S  O  D  H  S
R  B  L  O  N  D  O  N  B  R  I  D  G  E  S  H  H  A
C  P  U  D  D  I  N  G  L  A  N  E  Z  I  G  D  H  F
```

Find the following words in the puzzle.
Words are hidden → ↓ and ↘ .

BAKERS
CHRISTOPHER WREN
EXPLOSIVES
LONDON BRIDGE
HOOKS

KINGCHARLES
LEATHER BUCKETS
LONDON
SAMUEL PEPY'S
MAYOR
PUDDING LANE

SAMUELPEPYS
SYRINGES
THOMAS BLUDWORTH

Describe what is happening in the picture.

....

....

....

....

....

....

....

....

....

....

....

....

....

How Has Fighting Fire Changed Today?

Label This Picture Using the Words Below.

Hose, Fire Engine, Ladder, Fire-fighter

How has fighting fire changed today?

....

....

....

....

....

....

....

....

....

The Fire Triangle

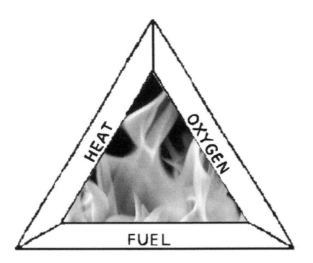

Fires need fuel, heat and oxygen to survive.

In The Great Fire of London, the fuel was the wooden houses, the wind provided the oxygen, and the heat came from the other fires started from the coals from the bakers shop.

To stop a fire the heat, fuel or oxygen needs to be removed.

How did they remove the heat?

....
....
....
....

How did they remove the fuel?

....
....
....
....
....
....

Fire Safety

Stop drop and roll is a way to smother the flames and stop it getting oxygen. These instructions were issued by the National Fire Protection Association.

STOP, DROP, AND ROLL - FLYER

If your clothes catch fire:

1. Stop
Stop what you are doing.

2. Drop
Drop to the ground.

3. Roll
Cover you face with your hands, keep your legs straight and roll over and over and back and forth to put the fire out.

Get help from a grown-up!

The most important thing to remember is to stay away from fire. It can catch your clothes on fire. Only use "stop, drop, and roll" if your clothes are on fire.

Smoke Alarms

During the Great Fire of London, Many lives were saved by the sound of the church bells warning them of the fire. Today all homes should be fitted with smoke alarms. For maximum safety they should be in every room, on the ceiling or high on the wall. They need to be replaced every ten years. When they chirp it means they need to have their battery replaced. You should test the alarms by pressing the button every day.

How often should fire alarms be replaced?

....

....

Where should you hang fire alarms?

....

....

....

How can you test the fire alarms?

....

....

What does it mean when it chirps intermittently?

....

Fire Extinguishers

CO2 fire extinguishers

These units use pure carbon dioxide to suffocate fire and leave behind no residue once the fire is extinguished. They were originally designed for class B fires, which are flammable liquid fires, such as oil, petrol and solvents, however, these days CO2 extinguishers are mainly used for the fire fighting on live electrical equipment such as televisions and computers..

Water fire extinguishers

These are used on class A fires of solid combustible materials, such as wood, fabric and paper. The water penetrates burning materials to cool down the fire, which extinguishes the fire and stops it re-igniting.

Which extinguisher should be used for:

A Burning Wood? ....

B Burning sofa?...

C. A computer on fire? ....

D Christmas Tree lights? ....

E Table cloth? ....

Design and Make Tudor Baker's House.

This model can be used as a teaching resource, it can also be made into a functional lamp and ornament.

There are a few different ways you can make this model. You can follow the advanced detailed instructions using foam board, which includes a lot of measuring and more suited to adults or older children. Or you can make it using three cardboard boxes and base it on the design, but do your own interpretation of what you believe the bakers shop in Pudding Lane looked like. If you are using cardboard boxes try get three different sized ones, so one will fit on top of the other one with a slight overlap. Then you can paint your boxes white, before decorating them similar to the model above.

If you want to make an exact replica of my model, please follow the following instructions carefully.

Equipment.

Most of the equipment is available from a Hobbycraft store.

- A3 Foam Board X 5
- A3 Black Foam Sheet X 2
- A4 Brown Foam sheet X1
- A4 Grey Foam sheet X 1
- A4 Clear acetate sheets X 2
- Permanent Black Marker Pen
- Ruler
- Foam Glue (I used two 2 fl oz bottles)
- Scissors
- Craft Knife
- Lollipop or cake pop stick
- Black thread
- Coloured plasticine or play dough.
- Blu tack
- Electric circuit equipment, including batteries, wire, bulb, bulb holder and switch.

Method.

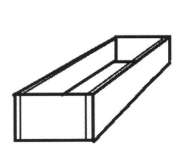

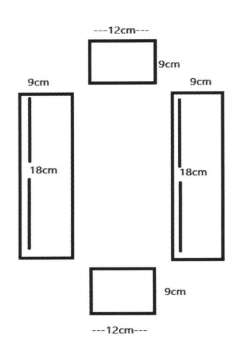

1. The base, Ground floor.

- o Using a ruler draw the above shapes using the measurements given on white foam board. Cut out carefully. If you are skilled at using a craft knife it is easier to do this using the craft knife, but make sure you have something hard underneath to protect your work surface from scratches. I used a chopping board.

- o Put the Foam glue on the outside edge of the smaller pieces and glue the longer pieces to these, holding the model in shape for a minute or two until the shape feels like it will hold together. The foam board is 0.5 cm thick so when made it should measure 13 cm x 18 cm.

2. The First Floor.

- o Draw the shapes onto foam board using the measurements below. Then cut them out carefully.

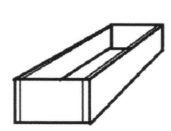

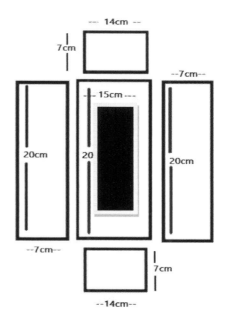

- o Put foam glue around top edges of walls on ground floor.

- o Cut a rectangle shape out of the floor to allow the light to reach higher levels from the bulb. Glue the floor (20 x 15 length) to the top of the ground floor, so it is overlapping evenly around all sides. The foam glue takes a little time to set, allowing you to slide the floor until it looks even.

- o Glue the walls to the floor taking care they are right at the edge.

3. The Roof.

- o Draw and cut out the shapes using measurements below.

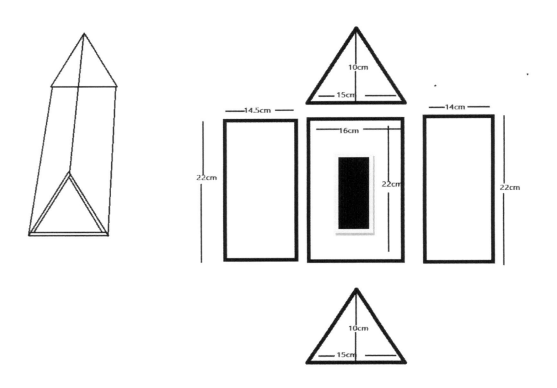

- o Cut a rectangle out of the centre of the floor to allow the light from the circuit to shine up to the roof before you glue the floor of the roof to the top of the first floor.

- o Glue each triangle to a few millimetres from the edge of the floor.

- o Glue the roof sides to the triangles. One is slightly longer than the other and should sit square with the other see diagram above.

4. The Attic

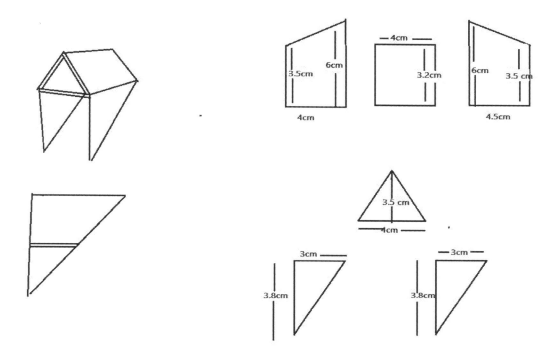

Draw and cut out the shapes using the measurements above.

The two 6cm sides are the pointy part of the roof .

1. Glue the triangle to the shape 4 x 3.2 so it stands up.

2. Glue the two roof sides to the triangle sides, one is slightly longer than the other to compensate for thickness of foam.

3. Glue the two right angled   triangles to the underside of the attic roof. Please see diagram above.

4. Glue attic to sloping roof.

Your model should look like this.

Leave it to dry fully overnight.

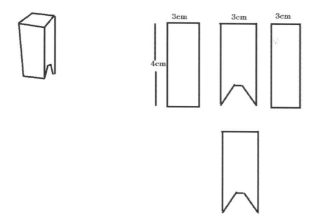

- o Make the chimney using the measurements above and glue together and glue to top of roof.

- o Draw where you want the windows with a pencil and ruler.

- o Cut out the windows with a craft knife.

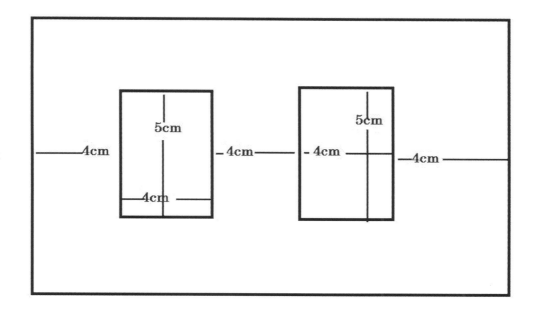

Th

Measurements above were used for my upper floor.

- o Once the windows are cut out, you can then cut out some acetate to a shape slightly larger than the window .

- Use a black marker pen and draw crisscross lines on acetate with a ruler. Glue acetate over the windows. You will be covering edges with black foam so don't worry that the acetate is overlapping windows.

- Cut out rectangle from roof just under attic window.

- Cut out acetate to cover attic window and also draw crisscross lines on before gluing it over attic window.

For the Bay window first cut out the window using the measurement of hole below.

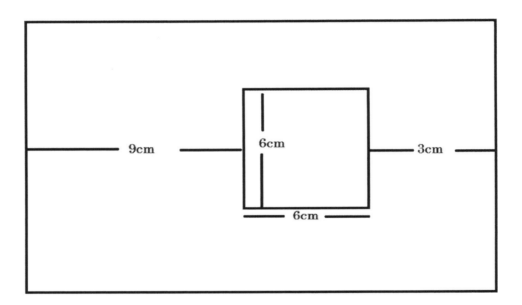

- Cut out a circle from the foam board which is 7.5 cm in diameter. Then cut circle in half.

- Glue half of circle to upper window, and other half to bottom window.

- Cut a piece of acetate to bend around semi circles around 7cm x 12cm. draw the crisscross pattern on using marker pen and glue into place.

- Make the door using black foam sheet, and strips of brown foam sheet.
- Cut out strips of black foam around 0.5 cm width and glue around edges of windows.
- Glue some strips around bay windows.
- Decorate walls with strips of black foam.
- Cut the grey foam into strips and then cut them into squares or rectangles. Starting at the bottom glue the foam along the bottom in a row, the next row should overlap them slightly. Continue and cover the whole roof.
- Cut a strip of foam for across the pointy part of the roof to neaten off.
- Decorate the chimney with strips of brown foam. Decorate the top with black foam.

Make some bread and cakes to go in the bay window using the plasticine or play dough, and glue into place.

To make the sign, use some black foam, type and print off the sign, and glue it to the black foam front and back. Thread some black thread through the sign and glue it to the lollipop stick. Make a small hole in the wall of the model and push the lollipop stick inside. Glue into place.

Your house is almost ready, if you want to turn it into a lamp, you can either put a torch inside, or make your own circuit.

Making a Circuit for the House.

Equipment.

- o Two AA batteries and battery holder.
- o Bulb
- o Bulb holder
- o Wire
- o switch.

Diagram of circuit.

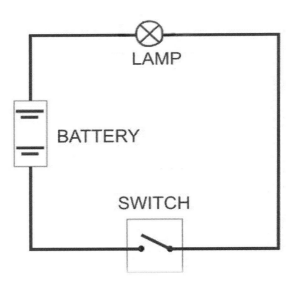

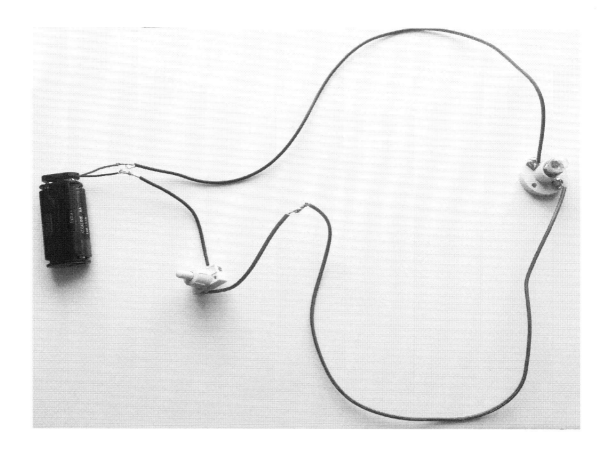

Decide where you want your bulb, it is possible to add two bulbs to this circuit if you wish, and have a light upstairs and one down. Once you have decided you can attach circuit securely. to a foam board base using either blu tack or sticky foam squares, or even Sellotape. The house can fit on top of the base. Experiment until you get your desired lighting effect.

Design a Gingerbread House - Template 1

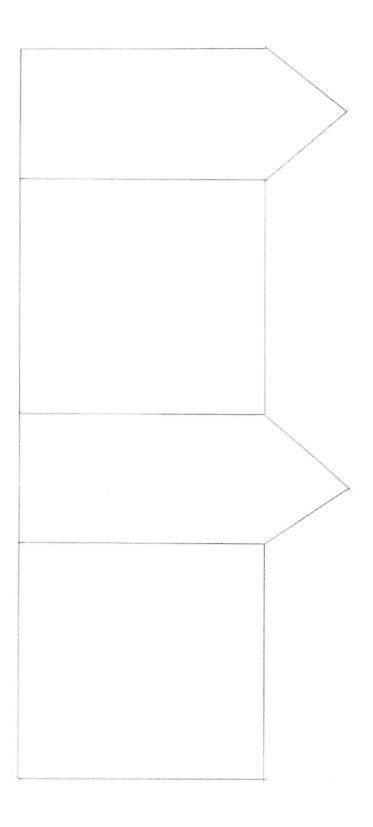

Template 2, For Gingerbread house.

(Not actual Size)

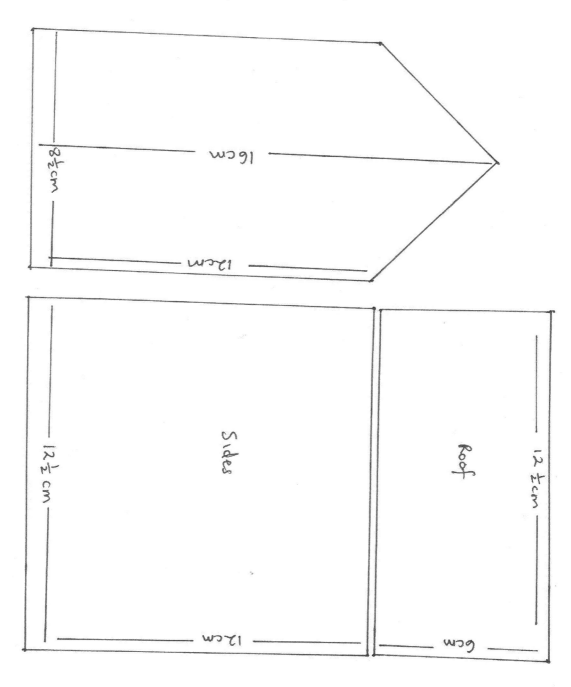

Recipe for Gingerbread Tudor House

Ingredients

- 375g Unsalted butter
- 300g Dark muscovado sugar
- 150g Golden Syrup
- 900g Plain Flour
- 1 tbsp Bicarbonate Soda
- 2 tbsp Ground Ginger

To decorate

- 500 g of Royal Icing
- 30mls water
- Packet or Black Sugar paste or Black ready to roll icing.
- Grey ready to roll Icing, or Packet of White Sugar paste and black icing dye.
- Some crushed boiled sweets or clear hard mints.
- Night-light candle

Method

1. First sketch your design using the design template 1 on page 48 like I have done here.

2. Preheat the oven to 200C/400F/Gas 6 (fan 180C).

3. Melt the butter, sugar and syrup together in a large pan. Sieve the flour, bicarbonate of soda and ground ginger together into a large bowl and make a well in the centre. Pour in the melted butter mixture, stir it in and, when cool enough to handle, knead to a stiff dough.

4. Divide the mixture into 6 equally-sized pieces.

5. Using the Template 2, from page 49, as a guide to sizes needed, draw with a ruler on paper the templates you need for the walls, roof and sides. Cut out the pieces.

6. Roll each piece of dough out on a sheet of greaseproof paper to ¾cm / ⅓in thick.

7. Using the cut out templates, place each of the templates on top of the rolled out dough and using a blunt knife cut around each template carefully.

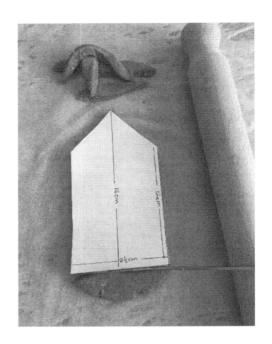

8. Cut out the sections for the roof, sides, front and back of the house. Slide onto two baking trays lined with baking parchment or greaseproof paper.
9. Next make a chimney shape shaping it with your hands so it has a sloping end, like the one in the picture and place it on the greaseproof paper.

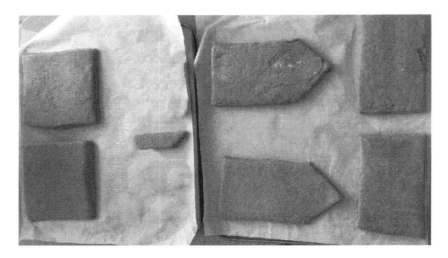

10. Tip - Keep any leftover dough, in case you make a mistake, you can re do one of the pieces.
11. Checking your design, cut a window out carefully from the dough using the blunt knife, and do the same for the other windows.
12. Place the crushed boiled sweets in the gap you made for the window. The heat should melt the sweets and they should fit the window as they spread out. Alternatively you could use a rectangle clear mint, and cut around it, removing the piece of dough, then placing the clear mint in its place. This will melt too.

13.   Spread your pieces apart in case they rise and stick together.
14.   Put your baking trays into the oven and cook for around eight minutes, then swap the two trays, putting the one on the lower shelf on the top, and vice versa. Cook for a further four minutes.
15.   Remove the gingerbread from the oven. Trim the edges so they are level.
16.   Leave to cool completely.
17.   For the icing, whisk the icing sugar and 30 mls of water in a bowl until the mixture is quite stiff. Put this mixture in a piping bag and use a medium plain nozzle.
18.   Practice putting the sides together, the two pointed ends will need to go on the inside of the two walls, for the roof to fit.
19.   Pipe icing along the inside edges of the walls, so they stick to the outside edges of the pointed walls.
20.   Press the four sides together and when stable allow the icing to set for around an hour.
21.   Whilst the icing is setting, prepare your decoration.
22.   Roll out the black sugar paste until it is very thin. Then taking a blunt knife, carefully cut strips of the black icing that will make your window frames and wood paneling, checking your own design and cut further strips as your design indicates.
23.   Roll out the grey ready to roll icing until that is also very thin. Then with the blunt knife slice it into strips, then slice the strips into squares, to use for the roof. If you are using the white sugar paste, then you will need to mix a little of the black dye into paste, kneading it until it is completely absorbed. You may need to add further dye to get the colour you want, but start off with a little dye first, as you can always add more. When you are happy with the colour roll out the paste until it is very thin, just a few mm thick.
24.   When your model appears to be secured by the icing, you can then pipe some icing on the sides and spread to cover the walls taking care not to go over the windows. This icing will also help your black sugar paste to stick.
25.   Checking your design, use the black strips of sugar paste, and decorate your model house.
26.   Pipe some icing along the edges of the roof pieces and position into place carefully.
27.   Taking each individual grey square, place them on the roof starting at the bottom edge of the roof, working along in rows.
28.   Roll a strip of grey icing into a long sausage shape and place it over the join in the roof.
29.   Put white icing all over your chimney, and secure it to the roof, holding it for a few minutes, and pressing it firmly into the grey tiles.
30.   Your gingerbread house is now ready to eat.
31.   As a special treat you could fill the house with sweets. Lift the house up carefully and push sweets underneath it before you put it down again.
32.   You can alternatively, put a night light inside just before you serve it. This will give a glow through the translucent sweet windows. Be careful not to leave the candle on for more than a few minutes, as the windows will melt and roof will singe. This should always be supervised by an adult due to the fire and burn risk.

Paint the Great Fire of London

Many artists have painted the scene of The Great Fire of London. The scene of the London landscape burning is dramatic and an event people want to remember.

Before you paint your picture, look at other artists impressions of the topic on the internet. Such as this one by an anonymous artist. In it you can see people fleeing the fire with their belongings. Notice how high the flames are reaching.

Now make a sketch and design your painting before you begin.

Silhouette of London Skyline Painting

Make a stunning fire painting.

Draw an outline of some Tudor buildings on black paper and cut them out. Cut out some windows.

Paint flames on a piece of white paper in red and yellow paint.

Stick your Tudor buildings London skyline silhouette on top of painted paper.

Design a T-Shirt

Design a T-Shirt with the Great Fire of London Theme.

Make Some Bread Buns

The fire started after the baker in Pudding Lane was baking bread. Have a go at making your own bread with this recipe for delicious bread buns.

Ingredients

- 500g/1lb 2oz strong white bread flour, plus extra for dusting.
- 2 tsp dried yeast
- 1 tsp salt
- 30g/1oz butter
- 75ml/2½fl oz warm milk,
- 225ml/8fl oz warm water
- oil for greasing
- Some rice flour for dusting

Method

1. Mix the white flour, salt and dried yeast in a bowl.

2. Rub the softened butter into the flour mixture until the mixture resembles breadcrumbs.

3. Mix the warm milk with the water.

4. Add the milk mixture to the flour mixture and mix together with your hands. Bring the dough together into a ball.

5. Using floured hands, knead the dough on a clean floured work surface for 20 minutes, or until the dough is elastic and smooth. Add a little more warm water to loosen the dough if necessary.

6. Put the dough in the bowl and cover with a clean damp tea towel or cling film. Leave it for 1-1½ hours in a warm place until the dough has doubled in size.

7. When the dough has risen, return it to a floured work surface and knock it back.

8. Separate the mixture into eight parts and roll each into a ball. Flatten each slightly with the palm of your hand and transfer the buns to a baking tray, placing them close together. Cover the tray with cling film and set aside for another hour, or until the rolls have doubled in size again.

9. Preheat the oven to 220C/425F/Gas 7.

10. When the rolls have risen dust them with the rice flour and transfer them to the oven. Bake for 8-10 minutes, or until golden-brown.

Make a Paper Tudor House

The next few pages have the templates to make a paper Tudor House.

1. Carefully cut around the house take care to go carefully around the tabs, do not cut them off.

2. Fold the house and fold the tabs backwards.

3. Glue the tabs together.

4. Cut out the roof.

5. Fold the roof and glue the roof to the tabs of the house.

6. Cut out the base and chimney.

7. Glue the tabs on the bottom of the house to the base.

8. Fold the chimney, and tabs, then glue chimney together.

9. Stick chimney on top of white square on roof.

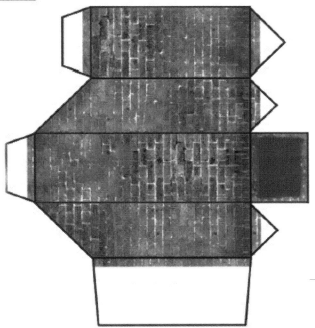

London's Burning Music Lesson

Equipment

Xylophones

London's Burning Sheet Music (On page 68)

Percussion instruments

Teach the song 'London's Burning' using the sheet music from the next page, giving every child a copy or put on overhead projector.

Demonstrate how to play the song on the xylophone.

Instead of singing the words, get the children to sing the notes. i.e. GG CC GG CC

Explain that notes are recognisable by their letters, and how they are written on the music.

Allow the children to experiment playing the song on the xylophone.

Explain if there is a fire, it is important to shout Fire Fire! Loud, so people can hear. Ask how they could make the word Fire Fire sound loud.

Show them some percussion instruments and ask them which ones would better be suited to the words Fire Fire. Try them out.

Sing the song again this time using some children to play it on the xylophone, whilst others use the percussion instruments to play during Fire Fire!

Ask them which instruments would be better suited to a water sound. Experiment with different instruments.

Split the class into four groups. Allow each group a selection of instruments and allow them to practice a performance.

Let each group perform their composition, whilst the class sing along to their music.

To end the lesson, split the class in half. The first half start off singing the first two lines, before the second half start from the beginning whilst the first half are singing the 3rd and 4th lines.

More able classes can be split into four groups to do this.

London's Burning

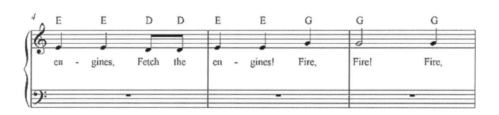

I hope you had fun learning about The Great Fire of London and using the activities in this book. Please leave a review on Amazon to let me know how the book worked for you.

Thank you,

Sarah Lee

Other Books by Sarah Lee

All available on Amazon.

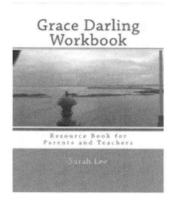

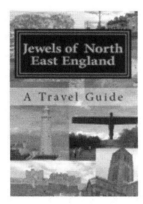

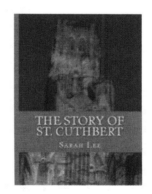

Printed in Great Britain
by Amazon